Let It Settle Journal

Let It Settle Journal

GUIDED PROMPTS *and* PRACTICES *to* MOVE YOU *from* CHAOS *to* CALM

MICHAEL GALYON

WILEY

Published by John Wiley & Sons, Inc., Hoboken, New Jersey.
Published simultaneously in Canada.

For general information on our other products and services or for technical support, please contact our Customer Care Department within the United States at (800) 762-2974, outside the United States at (317) 572-3993 or fax (317) 572-4002.

Wiley also publishes its books in a variety of electronic formats. Some content that appears in print may not be available in electronic formats. For more information about Wiley products, visit our web site at www.wiley.com.

Library of Congress Cataloging-in-Publication Data is Available:

ISBN 9781394259182 (cloth)
ISBN 9781394259199 (ePub)
ISBN 9781394259205 (ePDF)

Cover Design: Wiley
Cover Image: © nadtytok/iStock/Getty Images
Author Photo: Courtesy of the Author

SKY10084556_091724

Contents

Introduction

In many ways, *Let It Settle* is the book that I needed to read when I was going through difficult times in my life and feeling lost and alone. It's a collection of learnings that came from years of searching in many different directions and a lot of trial and error. My intention in writing the book was not to throw jargon at you to make you believe that the tools presented in the book, such as mindfulness, meditation, and somatic work, were worth trying but rather to give you an opportunity to experience the benefits while reading the book. I included tangible takeaways in each chapter to help you begin to embody the skill and employ it in your life when needed.

This guided journal is an extension of the book; its goal is to help you gain a deeper understanding of the tools presented in the book through practical application and deep reflection. Each entry features a gentle reminder and a key passage from the pages of *Let It Settle*. The journal requires you to look within your life and identify the areas where these tools would best serve you. I encourage you to take your time and include as much detail as possible in each entry. These pages are yours, and the story to tell within these pages is yours.

Some of the journal prompts may resonate more than others, and that's OK. Know that you can always return here as life shifts and you find yourself in need. My hope is that this journal becomes a companion for you this year and a space in which you can find yourself again.

As with all things, go slow, be gentle with yourself, and remember to take a moment to breathe in, breathe out, and let it all settle.

PART

I

Finding Calm

1

Letting It Settle

Just a gentle reminder . . .

Given everything that is happening around you, the concept of calm may be lost on you. The thought of stillness may seem foreign, and while you know that something needs to shift, you don't know how to move yourself toward a life of ease.

Letting It Settle Passage

Finding a space of calm is more necessary than ever. Between information overload brought on by social media and 24-hour news sources, increased demands for productivity, a breakdown of the boundaries between personal and professional life, and rising levels of stress and anxiety, it's essential to carve out moments of calm to preserve our mental and emotional health.

Writing Prompts: The Process of Letting It Settle

The process of letting it settle allows the mind to settle, the body to settle, and the emotions to settle so that you can move clearly through life and begin to see the beauty and safety that exists around you. As you work toward finding ways to let it settle, ask yourself where in your life you're currently feeling unsettled. Once you note the areas that are causing stress and anxiety, you can begin to implement the tools to help you get back to a settled space. Just as I learned from Jack, the preschool student I reference in Chapter 1 of *Let It Settle*, in order for us to settle into the present moment, we need to allow ourselves to draw awareness to those unsettled moments in our lives. Now create that space of presence for yourself and take a few moments to respond to these questions:

What situation are you currently experiencing that is causing you to feel unsettled?

_____

_____

_____

_____

_____

When you feel unsettled, how does it manifest in your body?

_____

_____

_____

_____

_____

_____

What emotional experiences are present for you in this moment?

_____

_____

_____

_____

_____

Why does it make perfect sense that you'd be feeling the way that you are, given everything going on around you and everything you've been through?

_____

_____

_____

_____

_____

_____

Using Calm Kit Tool #1: 5-4-3-2-1 Calming Technique for Anxiety

The best way to return to a settled space is to reconnect to the present moment. Take a few moments to ground yourself back into the here and now using the 5-4-3-2-1 Calming Technique for Anxiety.

Five Things You Can See

1. _____
2. _____
3. _____
4. _____
5. _____

Four Things You Can Touch

1. _____
2. _____
3. _____
4. _____

Three Things You Can Hear

1. _____
2. _____
3. _____

Two Things You Can Smell

1. _____
2. _____

One Thing You Can Taste

1. _____

After moving through the 5-4-3-2-1 Calming Technique for Anxiety, what has shifted for you? How have your mind and body settled?

_____

_____

_____

_____

_____

_____

_____

_____

_____

_____

_____

_____

_____

_____

_____

_____

_____

Letting It Settle Reflection Pages

After going through the process of letting it settle and writing prompts, take a moment to write what you're feeling and what came up for you.

_____

_____

_____

_____

_____

_____

_____

_____

_____

_____

_____

_____

_____

_____

_____

_____

2 Easing Anxiety

Just a gentle reminder . . .

There will be times when, despite your best efforts, no matter how many breaths you take, minutes you spend meditating, walks you take, or friends you talk to, the weight of your responsibilities will feel too heavy, and it will feel like you are fighting a losing battle against stress and anxiety. I want you to know when that happens, you are not failing. You are not a failure. It's just that in that moment, those feelings were stronger than the tools you have. You'll get stronger, and your tools will get sharper, but feeling overwhelmed in a stressful situation is *not* a sign of weakness. It's a sign that you're moving through life, just like the rest of us. So be gentle with yourself as you sharpen your tools and gain new ones. Know that sometimes the best thing you can do in the face of an anxious moment is allow it to be there without judgment or shame.

Easing Anxiety Passage

In those moments of anxiety, connecting mindfully to the present moment is a wonderful tool to start to find your way back to center. But as I learned at the beginning of my mindfulness journey, progress comes from consistency and patience. As you move through the anxiety that presents itself in your own life, remember to find ordinary moments to practice mindfulness so that you can begin to observe the world within you and around you and not allow yourself to be led by old habits and fears. And through it all, be patient and gentle with yourself.

Writing Prompts: The Process of Easing Anxiety

When facing anxiety, we are taken into an unsettled space where we tend to forget about the present moment. The practice of mindfulness allows us to find our way back to our current experience and leave behind thoughts of yesterday or tomorrow that invade during anxious moments. Over the next few pages, I guide you through the process of easing anxiety that I used when dealing with anxiety attacks and highlighted in Chapter 2. You will connect with a time when you felt a heightened sense of anxiety and explore what comes up for you throughout the process.

Connect to the Breath

Begin to explore the breath and write about how it feels. Get as specific as possible: What does the breath feel like as it enters and exits? What is the temperature of the breath? How does it feel in your chest, your belly, and so on?

_____

_____

_____

_____

_____

_____

_____

_____

Draw Awareness to Thoughts

What thoughts are present for you right now? Is your mind taking you into the future or the past? Are any recurring anxious thoughts present?

_____

_____

_____

_____

_____

_____

_____

_____

Using Calm Kit Tool #2: Body Scan

Bring your attention to the body. Begin to check in with each part of your body, noting the sensations and feelings that are present. Without trying to change or fix anything that is present for you, write down what is occurring as you scan throughout your body. (Refer to Chapter 4 of *Let It Settle* for a written Body Scan Meditation.)

_____

_____

_____

_____

_____

_____

_____

_____

Connect to the Heart

Take a moment to connect to the heart and ask yourself what emotions might be beneath the anxiety. Allow those words to flow onto the page and write about what you're experiencing as the anxiety begins to settle.

_____

_____

_____

_____

_____

_____

_____

_____

Find the Spaces of Safety

Explore your surroundings and begin to connect with the spaces of safety that exist around you. Write down all the things around you that can keep you safe and well.

_____

_____

_____

_____

_____

_____

_____

_____

_____

_____

_____

_____

Easing Anxiety Reflection Pages

After going through the process of easing anxiety and the writing prompts for this chapter, take a moment to write what you're feeling and what came up for you.

_____

_____

_____

_____

_____

_____

_____

_____

_____

_____

_____

_____

_____

_____

_____

_____

3 Facing Fear

Just a gentle reminder . . .

As you get closer to obtaining or achieving the things that are meaningful and important to you, a certain level of fear will arise. And at times that fear will become so overwhelming that you will want to stop before you take the next step, to rush back to safety and wait until the fear subsides. But in doing so, you might be waiting around for a long time. The truth about fear is that it rarely disappears with time; rather, it disappears when it is challenged by your resilience in the face of it. Recognizing that fear is there, allowing it to be there, and then making the conscious choice to step forward in the face of that fear isn't easy and won't feel good. But what you've been waiting for lies on the other side of that fear.

Facing Fear Passage

I like to think of our sympathetic nervous system as a protective parent on a mission to save us from the world we're living in. It constantly scans the playground and makes sure we don't fall from the monkey bars, scrape our knees, or get our feelings hurt by bullies. With each bump and bruise, our sympathetic nervous system becomes more aware of potential dangers and leaps into action in anticipation. But just as an overprotective parent often keeps children from growth opportunities and leaves them ill-prepared for real-life situations, so too can our overprotective nervous system, especially when it begins to sense a threat and push us into a space of fear.

Writing Prompts: The Process of Facing Fear

Moving through fear isn't exactly a natural response, and doing so will take time, patience, and the right tools. Let's revisit the steps that Caleb went through on that fearful night in Chapter 3 of *Let It Settle* and see if you can implement them in your life the next time fear pops up for you.

Recognize and Acknowledge Your Fear

Gently bring your awareness to the fear you're experiencing and allow it to be there.

How does fear show up for you? What does it feel like in your body?

_____

_____

_____

_____

_____

_____

_____

_____

_____

_____

_____

Observe Your Thoughts

In the face of this fear, what thoughts are present for you?

_____

_____

_____

_____

_____

_____

_____

_____

_____

_____

Identify the Source

Try to identify the source of your fear.

Is it related to a specific event, a past trauma, or an imagined future scenario?

_____

_____

_____

_____

_____

_____

_____

_____

_____

_____

Practice Acceptance and Nonjudgment

With the awareness of the thoughts and feelings associated with fear, give yourself permission to fully feel the fear without judgment.

If you were to talk a friend through this situation without any judgment, what would you tell them?

_____

_____

Using Calm Kit Tool #3: Butterfly Hug

Calming techniques such as the Butterfly Hug allow you to soothe the nervous system and remain in the present moment. (Refer to Chapter 3 of *Let It Settle* for the Butterfly Hug.) Take a moment to calm yourself using the technique, then write about the experience.

_____

_____

_____

_____

_____

_____

_____

_____

_____

_____

_____

_____

_____

Note the Spaces of Safety

To return to that space of calm, shift your focus from your thinking mind, which is alerting you to the threat associated with the fear, and find the spaces that exist around that will be there as you move through the fear.

What is currently within your space that represents safety and comfort?

_____

_____

_____

_____

_____

_____

_____

_____

Make a Conscious Decision

What choice do you want to make in the face of this fear? What is the next best step that is most aligned with who you want to be in the world?

_____

_____

_____

_____

_____

_____

_____

_____

Facing Fear Reflection Pages

After going through the process of facing fear and the writing prompts for this chapter, take a moment to write what you're feeling and what came up for you.

_____

_____

_____

_____

_____

_____

_____

_____

_____

_____

_____

_____

_____

_____

_____

_____

_____

_____

_____

_____

_____

_____

_____

_____

_____

_____

_____

_____

_____

_____

_____

_____

_____

_____

_____

_____

_____

_____

_____

_____

_____

_____

4 Meditations and Daily Habits for Finding Calm

The meditations and daily habits included in Chapter 4 of *Let It Settle* will help you find a space of calm in your life. As you begin the process of finding calm and incorporate these activities into your practice, use the journal to reflect on what came up for you after each meditation and how you plan to use the daily habits in your life.

Meditations

Body Scan Meditation

The Body Scan Meditation guides you through a systematic exploration of your body, from your toes to the crown of your head, bringing awareness to each part and noticing any sensations without judgment. This practice helps you develop mindfulness of your body, allowing you to release tension and stress stored in your muscles and tissues. Regular practice of the Body Scan Meditation can reduce anxiety, improve sleep quality, and enhance overall well-being. By cultivating awareness of your body, you can learn to respond to physical sensations with compassion and care, promoting greater relaxation and a sense of calm.

What physical sensations were present for you the most during the meditation? How did the Body Scan change your mood?

Four-Point Breathing Meditation

The Four-Point Breathing Meditation is an exploration of mindfulness and self-awareness that draws your focus to four key points connected to the breath: nose, chest, stomach, and edges of the body. During the meditation, you become attuned to the sensations of each breath cycle, from the cool air entering your nostrils to the rise and fall of your chest and the expansion and contraction of your stomach. With each inhale and exhale, you deepen your connection with the present moment, allowing you to take up space and feel grounded in your physical presence.

What came up for you during the Four-Point Breathing Meditation? How do you think you could use meditation in the future?

_____

_____

_____

_____

_____

_____

_____

_____

Safe Space Meditation

The Safe Space Meditation is designed specifically to help you find inner comfort and security during moments of stress and anxiety. By guiding you through a series of visualizations, this meditation encourages you to imagine yourself in a serene environment, ultimately leading you to discover a personal safe space where you can experience the familiar feelings of warmth and tranquility that exist in a real or imagined setting of your choice.

Describe the space of safety that you created for yourself in as much detail as possible.

_____

_____

_____

_____

_____

_____

_____

_____

_____

Daily Habits

Mindful Awareness

Cultivate a daily practice of mindfulness, where you intentionally bring your attention to the present moment without judgment. Doing so could involve formal meditation practices, such as the Four-Point Breathing Meditation or the Body Scan Meditation, or informal practices, such as mindful walking or eating, where you simply bring your full attention to the experience of common tasks that often are done without thought or attention. By regularly tuning in to your present experience, you can develop greater awareness and acceptance of whatever arises, which fosters a sense of inner peace and calm.

How will you practice mindful awareness this week?

_____

_____

_____

Mindful Breaks

Incorporate periods of mindfulness throughout your day to pause, breathe, and reconnect with the present moment. Doing this could be as simple as taking a few deep breaths before starting a task, practicing mindful eating during meals, or taking a brief walk outside to appreciate nature. Setting a calendar invite for a "Mindful Moment" throughout the day is a great way to reserve time to practice grounding yourself back into the present moment. These mindfulness breaks can help you navigate stressors with greater ease and maintain a sense of calm amid daily challenges.

Where in your life do you most need to take a mindful break throughout the week?

_____

_____

_____

Stress Reduction Techniques

Integrate stress reduction techniques into your daily routine to help manage the inevitable challenges of life. To promote relaxation and alleviate tension in the body and mind, include deep breathing exercises, such as the Four-Point Breathing Meditation; grounding exercises, such as the 5-4-3-2-1 Calming Technique for Anxiety (Chapter 1); the Body Scan (Chapter 2); somatic practices like the Butterfly Hug (Chapter 3); or guided imagery, like the Safe Space Meditation described earlier in this chapter. By proactively engaging in these practices, you can build resilience and cultivate a greater sense of calm in the face of stressors.

Which Calm Kit tools will you be using this week to help during stressful situations? How do you imagine they will help you?

_____

_____

_____

_____

_____

_____

_____

_____

_____

_____

_____

_____

_____

_____

_____

_____

PART II

Coming Home to Yourself

5 Listening In

Just a gentle reminder . . .

Not all of the thoughts that enter your mind are worth listening to. Sometimes completely nonsensical notions will race across your mind, but just because a thought is there does not make it true. At times you will experience automatic responses of negativity to stimuli around you. Unless these automatic responses are serving you in some way, you can discard them immediately. You can choose to step back and listen to these thoughts, assess their value, and allow them to pass if they don't serve you, just as you would with advice from a friend.

Listening In Passage

When I started to recognize these patterns of thought and realize that most were fear based and protective in nature, my approach to life subtly shifted. Instead of instinctively acting on every thought, I started to challenge the thoughts and really consider if they were worth listening to. When I started to catastrophize, I was able to stop and challenge the thought with a simple question: What if it went well? This shifted my focus from the worst-case scenario to the best-case one. Neither of these thoughts was based in reality, but one left me sleepless and the other filled me with hope.

Writing Prompts: The Process of Listening In

As you begin to cultivate awareness of your thoughts and observe them without judgment, you start to gain the ability to listen in and consider whether each thought aligns with your values and aspirations or if it pulls you further away from your desired path. Often our thoughts are merely automatic responses of negativity to external stimuli and conditioning based on the past. In Chapter 5 of *Let It Settle*, I walked you through how identifying my inner gremlin and personifying it helped me to see my inner critic for what it is. Then I could prevent the gremlin from making decisions for me. The following questions are designed to help you understand your relationship to thought and to develop a keen awareness of your own gremlin.

Label Your Thoughts

As you delve into your inner world, practice labeling your thoughts based on their patterns. Identify thoughts that replay past events, catastrophize future scenarios, or criticize your actions.

What thoughts occur most commonly for you and what type of thoughts are they (rehashing, rehearsing, catastrophizing, or gremlin thoughts)?

_____

_____

_____

_____

_____

_____

_____

_____

_____

_____

_____

_____

_____

_____

Using Calm Kit Tool #4: Gremlin Discovery Technique

Visualize your inner critic as a separate character within your mind, distinct from your true self. Give this inner gremlin a physical form or persona that embodies its traits and tendencies. By externalizing this voice, you create space between its criticisms and your authentic self, reclaiming control over your self-image.

Reflect on Inner Criticism

Begin by reflecting on times when you've experienced self-doubt, self-criticism, or negative self-talk. Think about the thoughts and beliefs that arise in these moments:

What was that voice telling you during those moments, and how did that message make you feel?

_____

_____

_____

_____

_____

_____

Identify Gremlin Characteristics

As you reflect on your inner critic, consider what characteristics or traits it possesses. Is it harsh, judgmental, perfectionistic, or fearful? Take note of any recurring themes or patterns in your self-criticism.

_____

_____

_____

_____

_____

_____

_____

_____

_____

Personify the Gremlin

Once you have a sense of your inner critic's characteristics, imagine giving it a physical form or persona. You might envision this voice as a small creature, a cartoon character, or even a familiar figure from literature or mythology. Get creative and trust your intuition. Have fun with this; give your gremlin a name and fully describe what it looks like.

_____

_____

_____

_____

_____

_____

_____

_____

_____

_____

_____

Engage in Dialogue

Once you've personified your gremlin, engage in a dialogue with it. You can do this through writing, visualization, or verbal communication. Ask your gremlin questions, such as:

What are you trying to protect me from?

_____

_____

Why do you say these things to me?

_____

_____

What do you need from me?

_____

_____

_____

Listen and Reflect

As you converse with your gremlin, pay attention to its responses and the emotions those responses evoke. Remember to approach the conversation with curiosity and compassion rather than judgment.

What insights or revelations arise when you engage in dialogue with your gremlin?

_____

_____

_____

_____

_____

_____

_____

Establish Boundaries

While it's important to acknowledge and understand your inner critic, it's also essential to establish healthy boundaries with it. Remind yourself that the gremlin's perspectives do not necessarily reflect reality or your true worth.

What are the boundaries you'd like to set with your inner critic, and how can you uphold them?

_____

_____

_____

_____

_____

_____

_____

Explore Core Beliefs

Listen closely to the messages conveyed by your inner gremlin, as they often reveal underlying beliefs about yourself. Reflect on whether these beliefs stem from fears, desires for approval, or feelings of inadequacy. Through this introspection, uncover the core beliefs that influence your self-perception and behavior.

What have you uncovered during this exercise?

_____

_____

_____

_____

_____

_____

_____

_____

Discern Worthwhile Thoughts

Amid the mental chatter, practice discerning which thoughts hold value and align with your values. Challenge yourself to sift through the noise, identifying thoughts that resonate with your aspirations. By consciously choosing which thoughts to engage with, you regain agency over your mental landscape, fostering clarity and purpose.

Which thoughts are no longer worthwhile?

_____

_____

_____

_____

_____

_____

_____

Make Conscious Choices

Embrace everyday challenges as opportunities for growth and self-awareness. Before reacting impulsively, pause and reflect on your values and intentions. Ask yourself how you can respond with mindfulness and intention rather than defaulting to habitual reactions.

What conscious choices are you willing to make moving forward?

_____

_____

_____

_____

_____

_____

_____

_____

Listening In Reflection Pages

After going through the listening in process and prompts, take a moment to write what you're feeling and what came up for you.

_____

_____

_____

_____

_____

_____

_____

_____

_____

_____

_____

_____

_____

_____

_____

_____

_____

_____

6 Cultivating Self-Love

Just a gentle reminder . . .

You don't have to change a single thing to be worthy of the things you desire. Who you are right now, in this moment, is enough. I hope that one day you will begin to see that perfection is not a requirement of a well-lived life and that striving for perfection and holding yourself back until you get there is only keeping you from the life you deserve. Stop for a moment and recognize that without a single shift in who you are, you are enough, you are worthy, and you are deserving of whatever it is that your heart desires. Stop holding yourself back by holding yourself to impossible standards and start seeing the beauty that is you.

Cultivating Self-Love Passage

So, what is self-love? It's the understanding that there is beauty in all of us. There is a beauty that exists in the broken and the bruised parts, the parts that are quick to anger, the parts that feel things so deeply, and the parts that can't quite seem to get it right. In spite of and because of all of those parts of us, there is goodness that

49

is worthy of love within each of us. And that goodness is not contingent on fixing or bettering any of those parts. Self-love is being able to look within without judgment and recognize that the perfectly imperfect being you are deserves love and kindness. The key to self-love is understanding that no amount of effort will ever make you any more worthy of love than you are right now. No deeds or actions will create a more worthy version of you, because worthiness is not dependent on anything but your mere existence.

Writing Prompts: The Process of Cultivating Self-Love

As with all things, there is a process and practice to finding a sense of self-love. I've found that utilizing this Self-Love Guided Visualization daily allows people to connect to the feelings of love and to replace the gremlin voice within. Over time, when that voice begins to speak badly of you, ask what your dear one would say to you. Just allowing that counter-point is enough to give you the awareness of thought and choose how to respond to it. By returning to the voice of a dear one and having their voice lead you, you slowly start to develop that voice as your own. People adopt the gremlin voice out of fear and external reinforcement of negativity; we can adopt voice of self-love out of care and consideration for our own well-being.

Using Calm Kit Tool #5: Self-Love Guided Visualization

Identify Someone in Your Life You Deeply Care About

Take a moment to think of someone in your life whom you deeply care about. This could be a friend, family member, mentor, or anyone who has shown you unconditional love and support. If no one comes to mind immediately, consider imagining a younger version of yourself or even an animal that has brought you comfort and joy.

Who is that person to you, and why are they so meaningful?

_____

_____

_____

_____

_____

_____

_____

_____

_____

_____

_____

Create a Daily Practice of Connecting with That Person

Make a commitment to connect with this person daily, even if it's just in your thoughts. Set aside a few minutes each day to think about them, express gratitude for their presence in your life, and reflect on the deep and meaningful connection you share. This daily practice will help you feel more connected and supported, even when the person is not physically present.

Where in your life can you incorporate this practice into your day?

_____

_____

_____

_____

_____

_____

_____

_____

_____

_____

_____

_____

_____

Utilize Their Voice as a Guide Toward Self-Love

During your daily practice, use the Self-Love Guided Visualization, described next, to connect with the affirmations and kindness expressed by this person. Imagine them speaking words of love and encouragement directly to you, just as they would in real life. Notice how their words make you feel, and allow yourself to internalize their loving messages.

What does it feel like to direct those words to yourself?

_____

_____

_____

_____

_____

_____

_____

_____

_____

_____

_____

_____

_____

_____

Combat the Inner Critic with Their Loving Voice

Whenever your inner critic pops up, imagine what this special person would say if they heard you speaking that way about yourself. Visualize them offering words of kindness, reassurance, and belief in your worth. Replace the critical voice with their loving and supportive words, reminding yourself of the love and acceptance they have for you.

What feels the hardest to combat? What messages are the inner critic still holding on to?

_____

_____

_____

_____

_____

_____

_____

_____

_____

_____

_____

_____

_____

Replace the Gremlin Voice with One of Love

Whenever you notice the gremlin voice creeping in, speaking unkindly or fostering self-doubt, consciously replace it with the voice of love and support from this special person in your life. Remind yourself that you are worthy of love and acceptance, just as they believe you to be. Cultivate a practice of self-compassion and gentleness, using their loving voice as a guide to greater self-love and acceptance.

How does the voice in your head change when you replace it with this reassuring voice of love?

_____

_____

_____

_____

_____

_____

_____

_____

_____

_____

_____

_____

_____

Cultivating Self-Love Reflection Pages

After going through the process of cultivating self-love and writing prompts, take a moment to write about what you're feeling and what came up for you.

_____

_____

_____

_____

_____

_____

_____

_____

_____

_____

_____

_____

_____

_____

_____

_____

_____

_____

7 Letting Go

Just a gentle reminder . . .

Whatever you're holding on to right now—whether it's a relationship, a job, a past experience, a grudge—if it's time to release the grip and start to create a life without it, let go. In letting go, you may experience fear, sadness, loneliness, or pain, even when you recognize that what you're holding on to no longer serves you. Know that those feelings aren't just from the anticipation of releasing that something or someone but also from releasing the future you had crafted for yourself in your mind. Go ahead and mourn the loss of that future. Let the sadness, fear, loneliness, and pain wash over you, and grieve for as long as you need. Once that grieving has begun, you give yourself the ability to slowly start to move forward toward a new future, one beyond your current situation that can be fully aligned with who you want to be in this world. It's there for you, but in order to get there, you need to let go.

Letting Go Passage

Often the concept of letting go is connected to a feeling of giving up. We're afraid that by letting go, we relinquish our power and admit to the world that we've failed. But letting go is not waving the white flag of defeat; it's detaching ourselves from the need to control the outcome. It's recognizing that without controlling, possessing, or excessively identifying with something, we will be OK. Letting go is a practice of finding freedom and inner peace by releasing the bonds of attachment that often lead to suffering and dissatisfaction.

Writing Prompts: The Process of Letting Go

Navigating significant life changes, such as divorce, the loss of a job, or the unexpected death of a loved one, requires acknowledging the loss of a once-cherished future while embracing the opportunity to redefine your path. The future-mapping technique outlined in Chapter 7 of *Let It Settle* guides you through a comprehensive process of mourning, reflection, and forward thinking, incorporating seven key aspects of a well-rounded life. Think of a life change that's occurred for which you are having a difficult time letting go of plans you had made. It could be the ending of a relationship, a friendship, or a job, or the loss of a loved one. Use the following prompts to guide you through the process.

Articulate the Current Vision

Reflect on the envisioned future associated with what you are letting go of, and write down the vision that you crafted for each of the next areas in your life.

Family: Describe the envisioned family structure, dynamics, and shared aspirations.

_____

_____

_____

_____

Career: Detail career goals, aspirations, and envisioned professional accomplishments.

_____

_____

_____

_____

Health and wellness: Reflect on health goals, lifestyle choices, and overall well-being.

_____

_____

_____

_____

_____

_____

Social life: Consider social connections, friendships, and community involvement.

_____

_____

_____

_____

Spiritual connection: Explore beliefs, practices, and the role of spirituality in your envisioned future.

_____

_____

_____

_____

Emotional well-being: Acknowledge emotional needs, coping mechanisms, and mental health considerations.

_____

_____

_____

_____

_____

Love: Describe the dynamics, aspirations, and shared experiences within romantic relationships.

_____

_____

_____

_____

_____

Reconnect with Your Younger Self

Visualize your younger self, free from current constraints, and recall past aspirations in each key area of life. Reflect on the dreams and goals you held for:

Family:

_____

_____

_____

_____

_____

Career:

_____

_____

_____

_____

_____

Health and wellness:

_____

_____

_____

_____

_____

Social life:

_____

_____

_____

_____

_____

Spiritual connection:

_____

_____

_____

_____

_____

Emotional well-being:

_____

_____

_____

_____

_____

Love:

_____

_____

_____

_____

_____

Integrating Past and Present Visions

Compare your current and past visions, identifying elements to retain and those to release in each key area of life. List the goals and dreams that you want to keep and those that are worth leaving behind.

_____

_____

_____

_____

_____

_____

_____

_____

_____

Craft a Future Vision

Envision a future that transcends the past, incorporating elements from both present and past visions in each key area of life. Describe your holistic future vision and dream in each of these areas:

Family:

_____

_____

_____

_____

_____

Career:

_____

_____

_____

_____

_____

Health and wellness:

_____

_____

_____

_____

_____

_____

Social life:

_____

_____

_____

_____

_____

Spiritual connection:

_____

_____

_____

_____

_____

Emotional well-being:

_____

_____

_____

_____

_____

_____

Love:

_____

_____

_____

_____

_____

_____

Detail the Future Vision

Set specific goals and intentions for each key area of life within your new future vision, ensuring balance and alignment with your values and aspirations. When you have a clear goal for each area, create a roadmap for achieving your envisioned future, incorporating actionable steps for growth and fulfillment in the key areas of life. In the space provided, write down the goal and the first step, no matter how small, that will set you on a path toward where you want to be in each of the listed areas:

Family:

Goal: _____

_____

_____

Step 1: _____

_____

_____

Career:

Goal: _____

_____

_____

Step 1: _____

_____

_____

Health and wellness:

Goal: _____

_____

_____

Step 1: _____

_____

_____

Social life:

Goal: _____

_____

_____

Step 1: _____

_____

_____

Spiritual connection:

Goal: _____

_____

_____

Step 1: _____

_____

_____

Emotional well-being:

Goal: _____

_____

_____

Step 1: _____

_____

_____

Love:

Goal: _____

_____

_____

Step 1: _____

_____

_____

Using Calm Kit Tool #6: Calm Space Visualization

Visualize a place where you feel completely calm and at peace. It could be a secluded beach, a peaceful forest, a serene mountaintop, or any other tranquil setting that resonates with you. Use all your senses to bring this place to life in your mind's eye. Then write a clear description of what your calm space looks like and how it makes you feel.

_____

_____

_____

_____

_____

_____

_____

_____

_____

_____

_____

_____

_____

_____

_____

_____

Letting Go Reflection Pages

After going through the process of letting go and writing prompts, take a moment to write about what you're feeling and what came up for you.

_____

_____

_____

_____

_____

_____

_____

_____

_____

_____

_____

_____

_____

_____

_____

_____

_____

_____

8 Heading Home

Just a gentle reminder . . .

In order to come home to yourself, you have to stop avoiding those parts of yourself that you feel aren't good enough. So often you're hiding not just from the world but also from yourself. You hope that if you push those parts of you down deep enough or keep them in the dark for long enough, they'll magically go away. The truth is that no matter how much you hide from them, those parts of you are still there, whether you shine a light on them or not, and they tend to grow even in the darkness.

Heading Home Passage

As you continue on this journey home, start to build that relationship with all the different parts of yourself. Not just the parts that feel acceptable, but those that feel shameful and dark, that you have locked away, and that you can't yet accept. Let them be there, get to know them, and let them know that they are a part of you and you're learning to love them.

Writing Prompts: The Process of Heading Home

The change doesn't happen all at once, but slowly these moments meet you through the conscious effort to return to a space of comfort, safety, and belonging. Coming home to yourself is a journey of self-discovery, growth, and transformation, and it involves creating a nurturing and supportive relationship with yourself. It's about reconnecting with the deepest parts of who you are and finding solace, strength, and wholeness within yourself. Start to examine those moments and see how they are showing up in your life.

Self-Awareness

Self-awareness begins by developing a deep understanding of your thoughts, feelings, and behaviors. Doing this requires time and attention and a great deal of introspection and reflection.

Pause for a moment and consider who you are in the world. Without judgment and with full honesty, start to journal on who you know yourself to be.

_____

_____

_____

_____

_____

_____

_____

_____

_____

_____

_____

Self-Acceptance

In self-acceptance, you embrace all aspects of yourself, including your strengths, weaknesses, imperfections, and vulnerabilities. Start to practice self-acceptance by acknowledging your inherent worthiness and deservingness of love.

What makes you worthy and deserving of love?

_____

_____

_____

_____

_____

_____

_____

_____

_____

_____

Self-Compassion

Self-compassion is the ability to treat yourself with kindness, understanding, and empathy, especially during difficult times or when facing challenges. One way to practice self-compassion is by extending the same care and support to yourself that you would offer to a dear friend.

What was the last kind thing you did for someone you deeply care about? What would it feel like to extend that type of support to yourself?

_____

_____

_____

_____

_____

_____

_____

_____

_____

_____

_____

_____

_____

Using Tool Calm Kit Tool #7: Self-Compassion Journal

As you write, consciously practice self-compassion by offering yourself kindness, understanding, and acceptance. Treat yourself as you would a close friend who is going through a similar experience. Use compassionate language and affirmations to support yourself.

In the next space, write yourself a letter of encouragement, letting yourself know that you see how hard you're trying and that you're proud of yourself.

_____

_____

_____

_____

_____

_____

_____

_____

_____

_____

_____

_____

_____

Authenticity

Once you've started to come home to yourself, you begin to live in alignment with your true values, beliefs, and aspirations. Your thoughts, words, and actions reflect that genuineness and authenticity, and you begin expressing yourself honestly and openly without fear of judgment.

Start to envision your authentic self fully at home in yourself. How would that version of you approach life differently than you do now?

_____

_____

_____

_____

_____

_____

_____

_____

_____

_____

_____

_____

Inner Peace

When you begin to show up in full alignment with who you are in the world, a sense of inner calm, contentment, and fulfillment comes into your life. You begin to let go of external pressures and expectations, focusing instead on finding peace within yourself and living in harmony with the present moment.

What is currently standing in the way of finding that inner peace and keeping you from coming home to yourself?

_____

_____

_____

_____

_____

_____

_____

_____

_____

_____

_____

_____

_____

Heading Home Reflection Pages

After going through the process of heading home and writing prompts, take a moment to write what you're feeling and what came up for you.

_____

_____

_____

_____

_____

_____

_____

_____

_____

_____

_____

_____

_____

_____

_____

_____

_____

_____

_____

_____

_____

_____

_____

_____

_____

_____

_____

_____

_____

_____

_____

_____

_____

_____

_____

_____

_____

9

Meditations and Daily Habits for Coming Home to Yourself

The meditations and daily habits included in Chapter 9 of *Let It Settle* help you gain a deeper understanding of yourself and find your way back home to yourself. As you read the scripted meditations, give yourself a moment to reflect on what comes up for you and determine how you can use these as part of your practice.

Meditations

Mindful Awareness of Thought Meditation

The Mindful Awareness of Thought Meditation guides participants to find stillness and return to the present moment by letting go of past worries and future fears. With closed eyes or a soft gaze, individuals focus on the breath, exploring four types of thought: rehearsing, rehashing, catastrophizing, and judging. They allow their minds to wander freely before labeling and categorizing thoughts without judgment. Through a brief body scan, participants redirect attention to physical sensations, fostering self-awareness and mindful redirection.

Where does your mind tend to wander in moments of stillness? How difficult is it to pull back into the present moment?

_____

_____

_____

_____

_____

_____

_____

_____

_____

Self-Love Meditation

The Self-Love Meditation is a practice that helps cultivate a deep sense of love, acceptance, and compassion toward oneself. Research suggests that practicing self-love can improve self-esteem, reduce anxiety and depression, and enhance overall well-being. By connecting with the unconditional love within, we can heal past wounds, release self-judgment, and embrace ourselves with kindness and compassion. This guided visualization offers a safe and nurturing space to come home to ourselves, reconnecting with the inherent worth and value that resides within each of us.

What shifted in you when you allowed yourself to say words of affirmation to yourself?

_____

_____

_____

_____

_____

_____

_____

_____

_____

_____

Heart-Centered Meditation

The Heart-Centered Meditation helps us connect with the wisdom and guidance of our hearts. Research suggests that heart-centered practices can reduce stress, improve emotional well-being, and enhance intuition. By tuning in to the wisdom of our hearts, we can access a deeper understanding of ourselves and our true desires. This meditation offers a space to come home to ourselves, reconnecting with the love, wisdom, and guidance that resides within our hearts. As we cultivate a deeper connection to our hearts, we can navigate life's challenges with greater clarity, compassion, and resilience, fostering a sense of peace and harmony within ourselves and in our interactions with others.

After going through the meditation, what desire called out to you the loudest?

_____

_____

_____

_____

_____

_____

_____

_____

_____

_____

Daily Habits

Daily Self-Reflection Practice

Daily Self-Reflection is a powerful habit that empowers you to engage in a dialogue with yourself, fostering self-awareness and nurturing a deeper connection with your inner wisdom. Dedicate a few moments each day to this transformative practice, carving out a quiet space where you can be with your thoughts undisturbed. Begin by grounding yourself with a series of deep breaths, inviting a sense of calm and centeredness in. As you reflect on the events, emotions, and experiences of the day, observe any recurring patterns, emotions, or areas of tension that surface. Pose open-ended inquiries to yourself, probing into your emotional, physical, and mental states. Express gratitude for the day's blessings, examine challenges faced, and extract valuable lessons from your encounters. Whether you are journaling or performing quiet contemplation, honor your reflections with gentleness and compassion, embracing yourself with kindness and understanding. Conclude your self-reflection practice by crafting an intention or affirmation that resonates with your values and aspirations, guiding you toward a path of self-fulfillment and growth.

Examples of open-ended questions to ask yourself and journal on are:

- How am I feeling emotionally, physically, and mentally?
- What am I grateful for today?
- What challenges did I face, and how did I respond to them?
- What can I learn from today's experiences?

What open-ended questions will you include in your Self-Reflection Practice this week?

_____

_____

_____

Daily Intention-Setting Practice

Setting intentions aligned with your vision for life empowers you to clarify your values, channel your focus, and manifest your aspirations into reality. Kickstart each day by immersing yourself in this ritual, seeking out that calm space where you can find stillness for a few moments. Ground yourself with a series of deep breaths, allowing the rhythm of your breath to anchor you in the present moment. Delve into the depths of your long-term goals, values, and aspirations, discerning what truly resonates with your desires. From this place of clarity, craft an intention for the day that aligns with your overarching vision for your life. Express your intention in the present tense, making it feel positive and powerful and as if it's already unfolding before your eyes. Envision yourself embodying this intention with clarity and conviction and lean into what it feels like to be experiencing this in life. Carry this intention close to your heart throughout the day, allowing its guiding light to illuminate your path and infuse your thoughts, actions, and decisions with purpose and meaning.

Examples of daily intentions are:

- Today, I intend to approach challenges with grace and resilience, knowing that each obstacle is an opportunity for growth and learning.
- My intention for today is to cultivate gratitude and appreciation for the abundance that surrounds me, recognizing the beauty in both big and small moments.

I set the intention to prioritize self-care and nourish my mind, body, and spirit with kindness, compassion, and nurturing practices throughout the day.

What are a few intentions that you might use as you build your Daily Intention Practice?

_____

_____

_____

Daily Acts of Self-Care

Daily acts of self-care are essential to nourish your mind, body, and soul and to create a sense of balance and harmony in your life. Make self-care a priority by scheduling time each day for activities that nourish and rejuvenate you. Create a self-care routine that includes activities such as meditation, reading, bathing, spending time in nature, or enjoying a hobby. Listen to your body and mind, and choose activities that replenish your energy and bring you joy and fulfillment. Practice mindfulness during your self-care activities, savoring each moment and fully immersing yourself in the experience. Set boundaries and prioritize self-care, even when life gets busy or stressful. Be gentle with yourself and let go of perfectionism, allowing self-care to be a nourishing and nurturing practice rather than a chore. Reflect on how each self-care activity makes you feel, and adjust your routine as needed to meet your evolving needs and preferences.

What self-care activities and routines can you add to your daily routine?

_____

_____

_____

_____

_____

_____

_____

_____

PART III

Honoring Connection

10 Understanding Empathy

Just a gentle reminder . . .

Each person you've met and every situation you've encountered has impacted the way in which you exist in the world. An entire life filled with experiences, both positive and negative, has crafted a specific lens that filters how you see the world around you. Every action you take and every choice you make is influenced by your unique lived experience. And just as you have your own lens that colors life in a specific way, every other human has their own lens.

Understanding Empathy Passage

In simplest terms, the word "empathy" refers to the act of putting oneself in someone else's shoes and being able to share their feelings. Empathy goes beyond mere sympathy, providing a passive acknowledgment of one's emotions and allowing for an active engagement with another's experience. Sympathy is a nod of recognition from a distance; empathy extends a hand and walks alongside the other through their joys and sorrows.

Writing Prompts: The Process of Understanding Empathy

Empathetic Inquiry Process

Use the Empathetic Inquiry Process when you are trying to deepen your understanding of a person in your life and to show up with empathy and compassion. Whether it's a friend, colleague, family member, or an intimate partner, this process can guide you.

What values and beliefs may be guiding their actions and decisions?

_____

_____

_____

_____

_____

_____

_____

_____

_____

_____

_____

What life experiences and background may have influenced their perspective?

_____

_____

_____

_____

_____

_____

_____

_____

_____

How may their actions or beliefs benefit them?

_____

_____

_____

_____

_____

_____

_____

_____

_____

What may support their beliefs?

_____

_____

_____

_____

_____

_____

_____

_____

Why would this decision or belief make perfect sense for them?

_____

_____

_____

_____

_____

_____

_____

_____

_____

What is the possible pain underneath all their behaviors or beliefs, and how can others show compassion and help to alleviate the person's suffering?

_____

_____

_____

_____

_____

_____

_____

_____

How has this process changed your perspective on this person?

_____

_____

_____

_____

_____

_____

_____

_____

Using Calm Kit Tool #8: Nonjudgment Practice

The practice of nonjudgment in mindfulness involves observing your thoughts, emotions, and experiences without evaluating them as good or bad, right or wrong. It's about cultivating a stance of open curiosity and acceptance toward whatever arises in your awareness, without getting caught up in judgments or criticisms.

> When was the last time you felt truly accepted by someone? What did they do to create a space of nonjudgment for you?

_____

_____

_____

_____

_____

_____

_____

_____

_____

_____

_____

Learning from their example, how could you create a space of nonjudgment for yourself?

_____

_____

_____

_____

_____

_____

_____

_____

_____

_____

_____

_____

_____

_____

_____

_____

_____

Understanding Empathy
Reflection Pages

After going through this process and writing prompts, take a moment to write what you're feeling and what came up for you.

_____

_____

_____

_____

_____

_____

_____

_____

_____

_____

_____

_____

_____

_____

_____

_____

_____

_____

11 Navigating Anger

Just a gentle reminder . . .

Anger is an uncomfortable emotion as it elicits such strong reactions to the situation at hand, but just because something is uncomfortable doesn't mean that it is bad. There are lessons to be learned from anger. When you learn to allow anger to be present in your life, you open yourself to fuller experiences.

Navigating Anger Passage

Anger comes from an activation of the sympathetic nervous system and is the fight part of the fight-or-flight response. That anger response leads us to take quick action to avoid a perceived threat. It's a very valuable tool when we are being chased by a bear in the wilderness, but it's not as useful when someone bumps into us in line at the grocery store. By using mindfulness to develop a conscious awareness of thought, feeling, and the impulses to action when anger arises, we can pause for a moment and assess the situation before taking direct action. A mindful approach to anger allows us to take control of our emotions and align our actions with how we want to be in the world.

Writing Prompts: The Process of Navigating Anger

Navigating anger is a challenging yet essential aspect of emotional well-being. In the face of life's challenges, understanding and managing anger can lead to healthier relationships, improved communication, and personal growth. By cultivating mindful awareness, clarifying personal intentions, and exploring the underlying emotions behind anger, individuals can learn to respond to anger in constructive ways that align with their values and promote positive outcomes. Through self-reflection, practice, and, when needed, professional support, individuals can develop the skills needed to navigate anger with resilience and compassion.

Using Calm Kit Tool #9: Anger RAID Meditation

The Anger RAID Meditation helps you approach anger with greater awareness and understanding. It involves recognizing, allowing, investigating, and determining next steps when you experience anger. If possible, bring to mind something that is currently causing you anger. Allow yourself to feel into that anger as you work through the next writing prompts.

Recognize Anger

Recognize anger. Ask yourself these questions, and describe, in as much detail as possible, your experience of anger.

What are the signs and signals that you are experiencing anger? How is your body reacting? What is happening to your breath? Where are your thoughts taking you?

_____

_____

_____

_____

_____

_____

_____

_____

Allow Anger

Allow anger to be present. Without trying to fix or make anger go away, allow that anger to sit with you for a moment. Witness how it expresses itself when you stop fighting against it.

What is the most uncomfortable part of allowing anger to be present?

_____

_____

_____

_____

_____

_____

_____

_____

Investigate the Root Cause

Investigate the root cause. Reflect on what specific thoughts, beliefs, or external events may have contributed to the emergence of this anger.

Are any unmet needs, past experiences, or habitual patterns fueling your anger?

_____

_____

_____

_____

_____

_____

_____

_____

_____

Determine Your Next Steps

Determining your next steps may involve choosing how to respond to the situation or deciding whether action is necessary. Consider whether expressing your anger directly, setting boundaries, seeking support, or practicing self-care would be the most effective way to address it.

What is the best next step that aligns with your values and supports your well-being and the well-being of others involved?

_____

_____

_____

_____

_____

_____

_____

_____

Navigating Anger Reflection Pages

After going through the anger reflection process and writing prompts, take a moment to write about what you're feeling and what came up for you.

_____

_____

_____

_____

_____

_____

_____

_____

_____

_____

_____

_____

_____

_____

_____

_____

_____

_____

_____

_____

_____

_____

_____

_____

_____

_____

_____

_____

_____

_____

_____

_____

_____

_____

_____

_____

_____

_____

_____

_____

12 Leading with Love

Just a gentle reminder . . .

One of the most powerful moments in life is when you discover that you do not need to be fully healed in order to experience love and that even in your brokenness you are worthy of receiving and capable of giving loving-kindness. When you can stop waiting for the moment when your healing is complete to enjoy life, you open yourself up to experience the beauty of the present moment in its entirety. Instead of seeing healing as a destination to reach before you can open yourself up to the love that exists, you begin to see that you are worthy of those experiences right here, right now. As you embrace your brokenness and vulnerabilities, you find a deeper sense of love for yourself and for others.

Leading with Love Passage

In the meditative practice of loving-kindness, or *metta* (from the Pāli language), the object of attention and awareness focuses on silent phrases that serve as wishes for peace, health, and prosperity. The intention is to move our default mode of thinking, which tends to be negative, toward a kinder and gentler tone.

Writing Prompts: The Process of Leading with Love

Loving-kindness is a meditative practice that focuses on silent phrases that serve as wishes for peace, health, and prosperity. The intention is to move our default mode of thinking, which tends to be negative, toward a kinder and gentler tone. In the practice of loving-kindness, those silent phrases are extended to different sets of people in our lives. Loving-kindness phrases are simple and organic so that the experience occurs naturally within you. They can be any phrases that resonate with you, but the traditional phrases are wishes for yourself and others to feel safe and well within their minds, bodies, and the world and to experience positive emotions and ease. Drawing awareness to how you respond and relate to the extensions of loving-kindness can help deepen the practice and give you insight into your connection with yourself and others.

As you move through the Loving-Kindness Meditation, take a moment after to connect with the experience using the questions listed.

Using Calm Kit Tool #10: Loving-Kindness (Metta) Meditation

Silently or aloud, repeat phrases of loving-kindness, such as:

- May (I, you, or all beings) be happy.
- May (I, you, or all beings) be healthy.
- May (I, you, or all beings) be safe.
- May (I, you, or all beings) live with ease.

Practice this meditation using the guided Loving-Kindness (Metta) Meditation script in Chapters 12 and 14.

Loving-Kindness for Yourself

Consider:

How does it feel to direct these loving-kindness phrases toward yourself?

_____

_____

_____

_____

_____

_____

_____

_____

_____

_____

_____

_____

_____

_____

Loving-Kindness for a Loved One

Think about these questions:

Whom did you choose to direct loving-kindness toward? How did the experience feel? How did it differ from the experience of directing it to yourself?

_____

_____

_____

_____

_____

_____

_____

_____

_____

Loving-Kindness for a Neutral Person

When extending loving-kindness to a neutral person, someone in your life whom you see often but do not know well, consider these questions:

What shifted in your perception of them? How did it feel to send those wishes to them?

_____

_____

_____

_____

_____

_____

_____

_____

_____

_____

_____

_____

Loving-Kindness for a Person with Whom You've Had Conflict

As you directed these words to someone with whom you have had conflict, ask yourself:

What did you notice about your feelings toward them? Did anything shift or change?

_____

_____

_____

_____

_____

_____

_____

_____

_____

_____

_____

_____

Loving-Kindness for the World

Ask yourself:

What did you experience when you shared loving-kindness with the world around you? What does inter-connectedness mean to you?

_____

_____

_____

_____

_____

_____

_____

_____

_____

_____

_____

_____

_____

_____

_____

_____

_____

_____

_____

_____

_____

_____

Leading with Love Reflection Pages

After going through the leading with love process and writing prompts, take a moment to write what you're feeling and what came up for you.

_____

_____

_____

_____

_____

_____

_____

_____

_____

_____

_____

_____

_____

_____

_____

_____

_____

_____

13 Finding Forgiveness

Just a gentle reminder . . .

There's a freedom that comes from being able to release the burden of someone else's actions. Anyone who has been hurt and wronged in life knows it's never easy to move forward and lean into forgiveness, but if the weight you're carrying is so heavy that it's impacting how you walk through life, it may be time to consider what unburdening yourself would feel like. Forgiveness is not necessarily for the other person but rather for yourself. It's handing back what has been on your shoulders for far too long and letting the person who has wronged you know you are at peace with the fact that the burden of their actions is no longer yours to hold. It's a process of uncovering your worth and recognizing what you deserve. There's never an obligation to forgive, but if holding on is costing more than letting go, it may be time to start the process of letting go.

Finding Forgiveness Passage

There is so much value in being able to put voice to your story and share it with a trusted source. When we've been hurt by someone, we tend to keep the whole story to ourselves and take on the burden. This is especially true with those we love the most who have hurt us. Our love for them can keep us from sharing their actions with anyone, because we fear that in telling our story, we will hurt them in some way. We would rather take on the pain than risk hurting them, even when they have hurt us deeply. But it's important for everyone to remember that our stories are ours to share. Holding stories in causes harm to no one but ourselves.

Writing Prompts: The Process of Finding Forgiveness

Forgiveness is incredibly important for our well-being and the health of our relationships. When we forgive, we let go of negative emotions like anger and resentment, which can otherwise weigh us down emotionally. It's not just about letting someone off the hook; it's about freeing ourselves from the burden of carrying around those negative feelings. Forgiveness allows us to heal emotionally, mend broken relationships, and grow personally. It's a sign of strength, requiring self-reflection, empathy, and humility. Ultimately, it's about moving forward with compassion and understanding, both for ourselves and others. If you're struggling with the ability to forgive someone or yourself, work through the following questions to help develop a roadmap for forgiveness.

Tell Your Story

Begin by acknowledging the weight of the emotions you carry. Holding on to your story can cause harm only to yourself. Consider starting a writing project or sharing your feelings with a trusted friend or therapist. By giving voice to your experiences, you begin the process of healing.

Take a moment to write the story that you need to tell.

_____

_____

_____

_____

_____

_____

_____

_____

_____

_____

_____

_____

Get Angry

Recognize and honor your right to feel angry about what has been done to you. Allow yourself to fully experience this emotion. Revisit techniques such as the Anger RAID Meditation (Chapter 11) to help navigate and process your anger in a healthy way.

What does it feel like to allow yourself to express anger?

_____

_____

_____

_____

_____

_____

_____

_____

_____

_____

Calculate the Cost

Take stock of the toll that holding on to this anger is exacting on your life. Assess whether you are allowing past hurts to dictate your future. Understanding the costs involved can motivate you to seek resolution and healing.

What has holding on to this anger cost you?

_____

_____

_____

_____

_____

_____

_____

_____

Determine the Value

Reflect on what you stand to gain by embracing forgiveness. Consider the possibilities for personal growth and liberation that come with releasing resentment. Visualize a future free from the burden of anger, and envision the positive impact such a future could have on your life.

What would be possible for you if you were to let go of this anger?

_____

_____

_____

_____

_____

_____

_____

_____

_____

_____

Create a Space of Empathy and Understanding

Shift your perspective to consider the circumstances and experiences that may have led the other person to hurt you. Cultivate empathy by acknowledging their struggles and fears. Recognize that their actions may have been driven by their own pain rather than reflecting your worth.

What does empathy allow you to see about this situation that you could not see before?

_____

_____

_____

_____

_____

_____

_____

_____

_____

Recognize Your Worth

Begin to acknowledge the toll that holding on to anger has taken on you. Recognize your inherent value and worthiness. Embrace the belief that you deserve healing, peace, and happiness.

Describe yourself as you would describe a dear friend, highlighting all the reasons you are worthy of all that you desire.

_____

_____

_____

_____

_____

_____

_____

_____

_____

Release the Vision of What Could Have Been

Acknowledge the loss associated with holding on to resentment. Allow yourself to mourn what could have been and let go of unrealistic expectations. By releasing attachment to past outcomes, you open yourself to new possibilities for growth and fulfillment.

What are you willing to let go of in order to move forward?

_____

_____

_____

_____

_____

_____

_____

_____

Envision a Future

Shift your focus toward envisioning the life you desire to live beyond your current circumstances. Visualize a future filled with joy, fulfillment, and purpose. Let this vision guide your journey toward healing and transformation.

Describe the future that exists beyond your current circumstances. Include how you plan on showing up in the world once you've released the burden that you've been holding on to.

_____

_____

_____

_____

_____

_____

_____

_____

_____

_____

_____

_____

_____

_____

_____

_____

_____

_____

_____

_____

_____

_____

_____

_____

_____

_____

_____

Using Calm Kit Tool #11: Forgiveness Meditation

The Forgiveness Meditation is a transformative exercise designed to release resentment, cultivate compassion, and foster healing within the self and toward others. Through guided reflection and deep introspection, this meditation empowers us to let go of past grievances, embrace forgiveness, and move forward with a sense of peace and liberation. Join this journey of self-discovery and compassion as we explore the profound power of forgiveness.

Reflect on Self-Forgiveness

Think about times when you have caused harm to yourself, either intentionally or unintentionally. Acknowledge the pain you have caused yourself, and recognize that holding on to this resentment is harmful. Place your hand on your chest as a gesture of self-compassion and say words of forgiveness to yourself. Allow yourself to let go of any guilt or shame you may be carrying.

What is something that you are not forgiving yourself for? How can the Forgiveness Meditation help support you?

_____

_____

_____

_____

_____

_____

Extend Forgiveness to Others

Shift your focus to people who have caused you pain or harm. Visualize their faces and acknowledge the hurt they have caused you. Recognize that holding on to resentment toward them only perpetuates your own suffering. Offer words of forgiveness to them, releasing any anger or bitterness you may be holding on to.

Whom are you willing to forgive for harming you? How will that forgiveness impact your life?

_____

_____

_____

_____

_____

_____

Seek Forgiveness for Your Actions

Reflect on times when you have caused harm to others through your words or actions. Acknowledge the pain you have caused them, and express genuine remorse. Ask for their forgiveness, and commit to making amends for your past actions.

Whom do you need to ask forgiveness from, and what amends are required?

_____

_____

_____

_____

_____

_____

_____

Release Resentment and Embrace Forgiveness

Take a few moments to breathe deeply and let go of any lingering feelings of resentment or anger. Embrace a sense of forgiveness and compassion toward yourself and others. Allow yourself to experience a sense of peace and freedom as you release the weight of past grievances.

What does it feel like to release past grievances? What is possible in your life now that you are not held back by resentment and anger?

_____

_____

_____

_____

_____

_____

_____

_____

_____

_____

Finding Forgiveness Reflection Pages

After going through the finding forgiveness process and writing prompts, take a moment to write what you're feeling and what came up for you.

_____

_____

_____

_____

_____

_____

_____

_____

_____

_____

_____

_____

_____

_____

_____

_____

_____

_____

_____

14 Meditations and Daily Habits for Honoring Connection

The meditations and daily habits included in Chapter 14 of *Let It Settle* are designed to enrich your relationships, fostering empathy, understanding, loving-kindness, and forgiveness. These tools will help to deepen your ability to be present in relationships, cultivating a profound sense of connection with the world around you. As you begin the process of honoring connection and make these a part of your daily practice, use the space below to share reflections on what each meditation brought up for you.

Meditations

Anger RAID Meditation

The Anger RAID Meditation provides a structured framework for acknowledging and processing anger in a constructive way. By *recognizing, allowing, investigating,* and *determining* next steps, you can cultivate greater self-awareness and emotional intelligence. This meditation encourages you to approach anger with curiosity and compassion, empowering you to respond to challenging emotions with wisdom and skill. Through this meditation, you can honor the presence of anger while also finding constructive ways to address its underlying causes and transform it into positive action.

What did it feel like to approach anger with compassion and allow for it to be present?

_____

_____

_____

_____

_____

_____

_____

_____

_____

_____

_____

_____

Loving-Kindness (Metta) Meditation

The Loving-Kindness, or Metta, Meditation provides a sense of relaxation and connection. Participants ground themselves in the present moment and visualize extending loving-kindness toward themselves, loved ones, neutrals, and those with whom they've had conflicts. This practice fosters empathy, understanding, and interconnectedness, promoting inner peace and enriching relationships. Research suggests that regular practice of Loving-Kindness Meditation can reduce stress, increase positive emotions, and enhance overall well-being.

Which group of people does it feel the most natural to extend loving-kindness to? Which group does it feel most difficult to extend loving-kindness to?

_____

_____

_____

_____

_____

_____

_____

_____

_____

_____

_____

_____

Forgiveness Meditation

The Forgiveness Meditation offers a transformative journey toward self-compassion and reconciliation. In a safe and serene environment, participants are guided through acknowledging self-inflicted pain, releasing grudges held against others, and seeking forgiveness for harm caused. Through gentle touch and affirmations, individuals embrace self-forgiveness, extend empathy toward those who have caused harm, and apologize for their own actions. This practice fosters healing, liberation, and a deeper sense of connection, empowering individuals to navigate life with compassion and understanding.

What does forgiveness feel like to you? What would change in your life if you were able to lean into a sense of forgiveness for yourself and for others?

_____

_____

_____

_____

_____

_____

_____

_____

_____

_____

_____

Daily Habits

Daily Exploration of Empathy

Transforming empathy into a daily habit can greatly enrich our relationships and understanding of others. Dedicate a few minutes each day to a perspective-taking exercise. Choose someone you want to understand better: a friend, family member, coworker, or someone you've had disagreements with. Reflect on their experiences, thoughts, and emotions, imagining the challenges they face.

Put yourself in their shoes, envisioning life through their circumstances. Practice compassion and empathy toward their journey, even if it differs from your own. Journal your insights or quietly contemplate, allowing understanding to grow naturally. Commit to repeating this exercise regularly to deepen empathy and broaden your understanding of others' perspectives.

With whom in your life do you experience the most difficulty empathizing? What would change if you were able to cultivate more empathy in your relationship with them?

_____

_____

_____

_____

_____

_____

_____

Daily Practice of Loving-Kindness

Cultivating loving-kindness can profoundly transform our relationships with ourselves and others, nurturing compassion, connection, and overall well-being. Create a daily habit of dedicating a few minutes to loving-kindness affirmations as bookends for the day, once in the morning and once before bed.

Settle into a quiet, comfortable space, allowing yourself to relax and breathe deeply. Silently or aloud, repeat affirmations like "May I be happy," "May I be healthy," "May I be safe," and "May I live with ease." Envision yourself surrounded by a circle of people sharing warmth and kindness. Extend these sentiments to loved ones, neutral people, those with whom you are in conflict, and eventually all beings. Let this start and end your day and be with you always.

If you were to create a new set of phrases of loving-kindness, what would they be? Why would they be meaningful to you?

_____

_____

_____

_____

_____

_____

_____

_____

Daily Practice of Letting Go

Establishing a daily habit of letting go involves dedicating time each day to reflect on past hurts and to release them. Find a quiet space where you can sit comfortably and without interruption. Close your eyes or soften your gaze, allowing yourself to settle into the present moment.

Begin by acknowledging any self-inflicted pain and releasing it with self-forgiveness. Then let go of grudges held against others by extending forgiveness to them. As you make this a regular practice, you'll find that it becomes easier to let go of resentment and anger, leading to increased emotional freedom and inner peace.

Over time, you'll notice a reduction in stress and anxiety as you cultivate a more compassionate and forgiving mindset. This daily habit not only benefits your mental and emotional well-being but also strengthens your relationships with yourself and others, fostering deeper connections and understanding.

What are you willing to let go of today? Make a list of the things in your life you are willing to part with.

_____

_____

_____

_____

_____

_____

_____

Final Thoughts

Let It Settle ends with a collection of lessons that I learned from the various teachers, students, clients, and loved ones who have impacted my life and helped shape the teachings in the book.

As a final thought for this journal, I'd like to share each of those lessons and then give you the space to add how those lessons resonate with you or apply to your life as well as a space to add lessons that you've learned from your own teachers.

Lesson 1: To find a space of calm, we need to first find a space of presence.

How this resonates and shows up for me:

_____

_____

_____

_____

_____

_____

_____

My lesson learned:

_____

_____

_____

_____

Lesson 2: The tools we need to find calm are sharpened through consistency and patience.

How this resonates and shows up for me:

_____

_____

_____

_____

My lesson learned:

_____

_____

_____

_____

Lesson 3: Fear is often an indicator that we're moving closer to the things that matter.

How this resonates and shows up for me:

_____

_____

_____

_____

My lesson learned:

_____

_____

_____

_____

Lesson 4: Just as happiness is not a destination to be reached, neither is calm.

How this resonates and shows up for me:

_____

_____

_____

_____

My lesson learned:

_____

_____

_____

_____

Lesson 5: We are not our thoughts, and when we become aware of them, we gain the ability to make conscious choices that are in our best interest.

How this resonates and shows up for me:

_____

_____

_____

_____

My lesson learned:

_____

_____

_____

_____

Lesson 6: Sometimes we need a reference point to return to in order to remind us of what true love feels like.

How this resonates and shows up for me:

_____

_____

_____

_____

My lesson learned:

_____

_____

_____

_____

Lesson 7: To move forward, we need to let go not only of the past but also of the version of the future we envisioned.

How this resonates and shows up for me:

_____

_____

_____

_____

My lesson learned:

_____

_____

_____

_____

Lesson 8: When you begin to come home to yourself, it doesn't come all at once, but through a series of moments.

How this resonates and shows up for me:

_____

_____

_____

_____

My lesson learned:

_____

_____

_____

_____

Lesson 9: While sympathy is a nod of recognition from a distance, empathy extends a hand and walks alongside another through their joys and sorrows.

How this resonates and shows up for me:

_____

_____

_____

_____

My lesson learned:

_____

_____

_____

_____

Lesson 10: There are no good or bad emotions, simply reactions to our circumstances that we get to decide to let guide us or not.

How this resonates and shows up for me:

_____

_____

_____

_____

My lesson learned:

_____

_____

_____

_____

Lesson 11: When we begin to lead with loving-kindness, we open ourselves to a deeper understanding of the human condition and see the humanity that exists in all of us.

How this resonates and shows up for me:

_____

_____

_____

_____

My lesson learned:

_____

_____

_____

_____

Lesson 12: There is a freedom to be found in letting go of the constraints of the past and forging a new vision for the future.

How this resonates and shows up for me:

_____

_____

_____

_____

My lesson learned:

_____

_____

_____

_____

I'll end this journal the same way that I ended *Let It Settle*:

Continue to be in motion, continue to trust yourself, continue to find your way back to center even when the chaos swirls around you. Remember that your peace is worth fighting for, and *you* are worth the fight.

And when all else fails, take a deep breath in, breathe out, and let it all settle.

About the Author

Michael Galyon has come to be known by many as their compassionate guide on the path to calm. With a kind heart and a deep appreciation for mindfulness, Michael serves as a nurturing presence in the lives of his coaching clients, his 1 million+ social media followers on TikTok (@coachmichael1) and Instagram (@michael.galyon), as well as listeners on his podcast, "Letting It Settle with Michael Galyon." Michael is a certified mindfulness instructor and professional life and business coach credentialed by the International Coach Federation. He is dedicated to creating a safe and inclusive space where individuals can find solace and cultivate a sense of calm amid life's challenges.

With an eclectic background in education, business, the performing arts, and health and wellness, Michael brings a unique perspective to his work and draws on his experience to connect with people from all walks of life. While his work may take him from boardrooms to meditation retreats, his mission remains the same: to help you come home to yourself and find a calmer, kinder, and more connected you.

Read more at michaelgalyon.com.

Index